AF886759

Soft Song

by Saundra Sharp

For all the Sistuhs who, having been alone too long, can still season their senses with smiles, and
sing
a soft song

Published for HARLEM RIVER PRESS by:
WRITERS AND READERS PUBLISHING, INC.
P.O. Box 461, Village Station, New York, NY 10014

First printing, Poets Pay Rent, Too, 1978

Notations of poems previously published:
This Last Piece of Paper — Johari (1975), Essence (1987), Crisis (1988)
Long Distance — Essence (1987)
Unfinished Puzzles — Johari (1975)
Thirty And A Half — Essence
For Those Who Tuned In Late — Coda
Changes, My Man?! — Black Collegian (1979)

CIP 90-071840

ISBN# 0-86316-306-8 Paperback
ISBN# 0-86316-301-7 Hardcover

ILLUSTRATIONS:
Kinshasha Conwill
Untitled, acrylic on canvas, 60 x 72 in. Page 45.
© 1978 Kinshasha Conwill
Tom Feelings
Untitled, pen and ink acrylic, 7 x 8 in. Page 24.
Untitled, pen and ink, 5 x 7 in. Page 48.
From the collection of the author
© Tom Feelings
Dadisi Mjenzi (Donald Fuller)
Untitled #2, from series, charcoal. Page 7.
© Dadisi Mjenzi
Mark Greenfield
Blessing, pen and ink and watercolor. Page 41.
From the collection of the author
© 1978 Mark Greenfield
Varnette Honeywood
Sun To Sun, acrylic on canvas, 24 x 48 in. © 1976. Page 11.
Birthday, acrylic on canvas, 22 x 32 in. © 1978. Page 22.
Watts Renaissance, acrylic on canvas, 48 x 48 in. ©1978. Page 36.
Double Dare, acrylic on canvas, 48 x 48 in. Page 43.
From the collection of Dr. and Mrs. James W. Hobbs, Los Angeles, California
© Varnette P. Honeywood, Black Lifestyles
Sylvia M. Miller
Winter Mood, enamel on corten steel, 15 x 16 in. Page 56.
From the collection of Ms. Rita Conyers, Elyria, Ohio
© Sylvia M. Miller 1978
Alfonzo Washington
October '77, pen and ink, 12 x 15 in. Page 35.
From the collection of the author
© 1977 Alfonzo Washington
Grace Williams
Helping Hand, glass mosaic, 24 x 24 in. Page 38.
Untitled, glass mosaic. Page 51.
© Grace Williams

Cover Drawing by Carlos Michael Cobbs

30

THIRTY

Well, I made it. Feels good.
Looking back, it wasn't so bad.

Looking back, it wasn't quite
how I'd imagined it would be.

The dot of gray becomes a patch,
becomes a stream,
And when they picture me sophisticated
I laugh inside,
remembering what I once thought
a Sophisticated Lady was
and did
and how glad I am
to have created my own definition.

Alone
has been fulfilling
and a bitch to live through
a necessity for the mind that creates at seven a.m.
a blessing when it was by choice,
a sign when it was not
an exhilaration in those few particular moments
when I could face it without fear.

Always the scrutiny,
and then the balloting—
Who shall penetrate my weaknesses?
and who shall not.
Who can be trusted with my sweet dreams
in this small place,
this secret space with room for few.

I have watched The Revolution start,
then start again,
and too many times
here and there,
in the face of a mother,
in the hopeless shoulders of a young Brother
I saw it end.
A pause,
then a voice saying
"Shall we try again?"

I had wanted to say
when I saw this day
That I had loved just one good man
But that would not be true,
because I thought it was him
and then I knew it was you
and now you're not here
But I am.
Maybe that's a blessing, maybe not.
Maybe just part of nature's plan
to keep a woman together.
Because climbing down is so much easier
than going up.

Well, I made it. Feels good.
Looking back, it wasn't so bad.

Looking back, it wasn't quite
how I'd imagined it would be.

Bring on the next thirty. . .
These,
in time,
Will probably become fine.

December 21st

SOFT SONG

Can I sing you a soft song?
Just a gentle soft song?
Woman soft, coming to you,
Wants to help you do what you gotta do.
Can I sing you a soft song?

I've been through some bitchy days,
I've shown you some loud and stubborn ways.
My mama said you weren't good enough for me
And you know just how badd I can be!

I put food on the table
When you couldn't find work,
And I remind you about those times
Even though I know it hurts.
Of course, you weren't no angel,
We both know that's a fact—
Sometimes when I tried to help
You told me to get off your back!

But this is a different day,
And it calls for a different song,
I've got to find a softer way
To let you know I love you—
I've loved you all along.

Can I sing you a soft song?
Just a gentle love song?
Woman soft, coming to you,
Wants to help you do what you gotta do.
Can I sing you a sweet soft song?

LONG DISTANCE

Woke up early this morning

Tried to reach you

Tried to slip into your sleep

and be a dream.

Make you turn over

smiling

and squeeze the pillow.

Tried to awaken your body,

your feeling,

your love line

And plant soft kisses

on your forehead and eyelids.

Could you tell I was there?

RETURN TO LINCOLN CENTER

I bring my smiles
and joy
to you today

Remembering when parks were a
safety valve
where no one knew
and no one asked
why the tears flowed

Remembering when I brought my
pain and misunderstandings
evenings when I
wished on the chandeliers
asked the fountain for answers

I bring exultation today
prancing tip-toe across bronze leaves
for your love has taken root in my soul
and parks
and you
and Lincoln Center
and me
are
places
and beings
for
music
and
laughter
and
love

as we grow season by season.

10/72

UNFINISHED PUZZLES

You are another of the
unfinished puzzles
of my life

I find myself
questioning
what you were all about
sifting
through the parts of you
I never knew
wondering
why I never understood

You are another of the
unfinished puzzles
of my life
I am the border
and you are
the missing piece.

Dadisi Mjenzi

FOR THOSE WHO TUNED IN LATE

(for Eubie Blake)

For those who tuned in late,
This is Eubie Blake.
Baltimore gave him his name,
But New York is where he sought his fame.

The Peabody Institute rues the day
That they chased little Eubie away—
Said he couldn't walk down their street,
But Eubie Blake didn't know defeat.

He started wriggling those fingers at the age of six,
And by seventeen was a professional hit.
He was "Wild About Harry",
And filled with "Memories Of You",
And did a little number for the Blackbirds, too.

Shuffle Along, now! you're really late
If you're just learning about Eubie Blake.
With Noble Sissle, and Miller and Lyles
He kept Broadway's patrons filling the aisles.

For those who tuned in late,
This is Eubie Blake.
Vaudeville was his musical game, and
He helped give ragtime it's claim to fame.

After writing a lot of songs
That still make us smile,
You'd think young Eubie would rest a while.
But he went to school
To learn some new tricks
And graduated from college at the age of sixty-six.

Twenty years later someone realized
It was past time that Eubie cut some sides.
The fingers still agile, the touch still light,
He cut an album that is out of sight!
(For those who tuned in late, it's called
"Eighty-Six Years of Eubie Blake")

Having crossed ninety, and still very young,
You'll find him performing or out having fun.
So we should all take a moment to sing his praises
And to say "thank-you" for all the music he gave us.

For those who tuned in late,
This is the gifted,
the brilliant,
the beautiful
Eubie Blake.

3/73

CAN I BE YOUR POET?

Hey!
Can I be your poet?

You have a doctor to call
when you're not feeling good,
And a lawyer when you need
a legal guide
do you have a poet?

You got the nearby cleaners,
and the local grocers
and the corner wine store
how 'bout a poet?

You got a teacher
And a preacher
And maybe even a analyst
(that you think we don't know about)

but do you have a poet?

a private poet for your mind,
a poet for your soul.

Can I, hunh?
Can I, hunh?
Can I ?

VARNETTE P. HONEYWOOD

BALTIMORE BUS CO.

If I was where I need to be
I'd get so much more done.
But I spend almost half the day
Just getting to and from.

When will someone realize
That I have poems and plays to write,
And minds to change, and other things
To set the world a-right.

Today, when I've no time to lose,
Things seem quite unjust:
Life is awaiting my next move,
But I'm stuck waiting for this bus!

GET UP AND WENT

(from The Sistuhs)

I got up this morning 'bout half past six,
And got ready to start the day.
Went to the bathroom to wash my teeth
And get last night off my face:
A roach big as me was sitting on the sink,
And it crossed my mind that he wasn't payin' no rent!
It made me so angry when I stopped to think,
That my get-up-and-go——got up and went!
Chasing roaches, no hot water,
Leaks here, there, everywhere,
And the hurrieder I go, the behinder I get,
'Cause my git-up-and-go, got up and went!

When I step in the kitchen of dear miss ann
After they done partied all night,
It looks like a disaster on the morning after!
Honey, let me tell you, it's a sight!
All the rest I got the night before
Just seems to go right out the door.
I look at that mess, and I confess
My cleaning pace becomes a snail's race
And the hurrieder I go, the behinder I get
'Cause my git-up-and-go, got up and went!

And that's just how I feel everytime I shop,
When I look at them prices
That done grown right to the top.
My stomach says go,
But my pocketbook says stop.
Tryin' to stretch them dimes,
Read between the lines,
Runnin' from store to store——
I don't like shopping no more!   'Cause
The hurrieder I go, the behinder I get
It makes my git-up-and-go, get up and went!

Now I was comin' home from Sarah's about seven p.m.,
And this big ol' thing come grabbing at my chin.
Said, "This is a mugging! Give me everything you got!"
Well, honey, I gave it to him with my pocketbook——Whop!!
Right upside his head! Then I got scared, you know,
And if I ever used some "git-up-and-go"
It was to get up and went from that scene.
I got my ass out of there,
Like I'm about to do right now.
Oh, but it just seems like
The hurrieder I go, the behinder I get
'Cause my git-up-and-go——got up and went!

My elementary school teacher assigned us to write a poem.
He then gave me a grade of 6——out of a possible 10 points.
I never could understand what happened to those other 4 points!
After all, I thought angrily, they were my thoughts, not his.
It was my love affair with poetry. . . . .

Sharp, Saundra
English IV - 6 per.
Mr. Neff

February 24, 1958

Poetry

Poetry.
It sings, it talks, it dances.
It does so many things.
And when I'm in a mood of gray
It lifts me on its wings to lands far
beyond my reasoning!
Poetry.
It explains the inexplicable,
Oblivious to the impossible.
And all my feelings pent inside
Are let run free and wild with every
syllable——
Poetry.

6 poems later I realized that you were not going to call. . . . . .

- 1 -

But I know.

I know that you could make me

smile inside

the way you make me

laugh out loud.

I know there is something in you

that wants to be gentle,

to reach out to play with me

as you would a kitten.

I know there is more

love in you

than music,

And

all that energy you

briskly manipulate

into movements of

being cool

should be exploding in me.

I would tell you what I know,

but you are too busy

working /

so very hard /

at being happy /

by

yourself.

\- 2 -

Not yet, you say?

Career, of course.

Apartment looks great!

And some other goals, too?

And she remarried, you say.

No more alimony payments, huh?

Feels good, I bet.

Just a half-glass will do.

Yes, remember, I saw you there.

I never believed that was true!

I didn't think you noticed.

Oh, he and I broke up long ago.

Well, I haven't danced in years.

Uh, no thanks, not tonight.

- 3 -

No, you see,

you don't understand.

It's not that i'm running from

You

i'm only running from my fears

While being drawn toward my needs

And i haven't decided which

one of those You are.

- 4 -

You are so deeply entrenched

in your bachelorness

that I wonder if you are

ever alone.

And when you're with her,

are you ever lonely?

- 5 -

One of us should be cooking

"dinner for two"

instead of

you fixing dinner for you

and me fixing

Dinner for two:

myself today,

and myself tomorrow.

- 6 -

I've been looking

all over my life for you

And here you are,

wishing I hadn't found you.

Oh, well.

I'll pretend I didn't see you.

Gonna go sit in Riverside Park

and watch the sun sets.

Until you're ready to be found.

Again.

TO ALL COLORED DISC JOCKEYS

How dare you interrupt Aretha
Just to tell me your name!
Or have the nerve to talk to me
While Barry is running down his game.

Stevie didn't sweat over "Sunshine"
So you could start the news
Before he sings the last line.
And I know what station I'm listening to!
If you got to remind me,
Then wait 'til Gladys gets through.

Recording is not easy, dear D.J.
And when the artist really has something to say
Then I want to hang on to every line—
Don't stop the music to tell me the time.

If Nick and Valerie want to give me something real
Then let me get it all.
Cutting in on them just to give me your spiel
Ought to be against the law.

I mean, how dare you interrupt Aretha
Just to tell me your name!

33 1/3

I NEED ALL THE HELP I CAN GET

House a mess
water like ice
laundry ain't through
got to buy food
exterminator due
and the cleaners, too
too damn much to do!

But when Aretha's in Paris
I'm in the front room
by the time she sings "call me"
I'm really pushin' that broom
this cleanin' scene is over real soon
and Lord knows
I need all the help I can get!

Ebony woman that I am
keeping straight ahead
tippin' tall
talk to me
sing to me
Billy Paul
keep on talkin' to me
'bout being soft
tell me Sister Sonia
'bout the queen I am
'bout walking queenly
in this unclean land.
Talk to me 'til I am
what you say I be
I know I need you
must read you
got to heed you
'cause
I need all the help I can get!

Diggin' on Malcolm's and Gregory's rap
filled my mind with their knowledge
of where it's at.
Diggin' on my people
pushed around
forced to play down
held to the ground
but hangin' on
so strong
that we're still movin' on
so deep
that everybody sings our song
but
we don't need no music   unh-unh
we don't need no music   unh-unh
we don't need no music   unh-unh

'Cause in checkin' it out
I see
I have all the help I can use
with a little left over
to give to you!

VARNETTE P. HONEYWOOD

THIS LAST PIECE OF PAPER

(for Grandfather)

It said that he was seventy-eight,
Born on a reservation,
Raised another place.

I sat there thinking that
I knew the exact time
Nat Turner struck out,
Sojourner Truth's life history,
When Phyllis Wheatley wrote her first poem
and why.

But until they handed me
This last piece of paper
to be filed on him
I didn't know
That he was a master musician,
A legal scholar who could not perform
in the courts he had prepared for.

Perhaps I have been studying the
Wrong brown faces,
For I knew only his pain and his love.
There was more I never learned—
Something that was him, and
much of me.

His moon and his music are in me.
His chess game with life's forces is mine.
And this blacknessance will not include
His deeds for children to marvel at.
They will not adopt his name.

So many questions I might have asked.
Such verbal treasures
That could have been unfolded to me.
But time has moved on.
This paper I hold
Knows all that I know
and nothing more.

April, '74

tom feelings

BE YOUR WOMAN?

Be your woman?
Would I be your woman?
I am your woman
holding my own
smiling most times
demanding sometimes
giving all times
giving all time to
be your woman.

Be your woman?
I am your woman
Waiting on you
Sometimes I think half my life is
waiting on you
you being late
you being "tied up"
you asleep with the TV
you not being here at all
Be your woman
is being glad to see you when you get here
like I waited for you
waited for you to say "love you"
waited for you to say "will you"
didn't wait to say I would
be your woman.

Loving you is
listening to your dreams
the pain of your realities
painful joy
restraint
restraining from saying some things
joy holding in and breaking free
freedom in being a woman
that a woman only knows
when she knows she is loved.

Be your woman?
I am yours in spite of you
There is no other way to be.

SATURDAY NIGHTS & SUNDAY MORNINGS

- 1 -

Definition

HOME:

is

wherever you

want to be

when nighttime comes.

- 2 -

Smiled at the moon,
The moon said "hi"
You're gonna meet
A sweet one tonight.
Then he winked at me
And I winked, too.
Sure am glad
The moon picked you!

- 3 -

Look Out!   The lady's in love again.

I had put away all my romantic dresses
I was about to succumb to the daily stresses
When a long-time friend said he was turning lover
And his plan was too strong——I couldn't run for cover. . .

Look out!   The lady's in love again.
I say, Hey!   The lady's in love again.

I didn't think I could feel love anymore
I really didn't want to open up that door
But my friend said he was tired of biding his time,
Now he was gonna put a sweet thing on my mind,
And he did!
And look out!   The lady's in love again.
I say, Hey!   The lady's in love again!

- 4 -

The magic of the first time is still glowing
In fact, I think it's showing (blush)

I smile a lot.

- 5 -

You woke me up this morning——

with your touch

your hands
strolling down my back
around my hips
your lips
saying good mornin'
to my breasts. . . . .

I reached for you

my fingers to push through your hair,
my palm to touch the softness of your face

but you weren't there

I felt you kiss my eyelids
before you slipped away

and when they opened,

a smile
tumbled
down
to
my lips

and lingers there. . . . .

- 6 -

Warm is all around me,
since I uncurled from your arms
to let you go to Work.

Warm softness is a cloth
from which I sew a thought of you.

- 7 -

feline infinity eagle
is but a humming robin bird
in love with the sun

u are the eagle
you can make silhouettes against your moon
the eagle's strength is in the words of his song,
the humming bird when she sings

You will always know their song,
for when they spread their
unmatched wings
they can look directly into each other's

eyes

and

fly!

A SENSE OF RELIEF

After I've bitched at you
silently
And at myself
out loud
And cried through the house
condemning the tears
for being so uncool as to fall
And repeated imagined desired
conversations with you
for the seventh eleventh time
editing with each round
After fighting not to call you
not to request your presence
After succumbing to the puzzlement of
why is it all going down this way
again
and why me! gods why me!?
And wondering how many nights
before sleep will come again
even with its void
After all the trauma of not understanding
you
us
You come quietly and ask to talk——
"to communicate," you put it
Suddenly
even before the dialog begins
Everything is so
gonna be all right cool.
Whew!

BREAKING UP

I'll keep the pillows.

Let him have the radio.

Who gets our favorite album?

I packed his shirt and his
toothbrush

His shaving cream

and the card
I gave him for his birthday.

He gave me back my sweater

and my small skillet

And part of the money he borrowed
when we went out last Friday.

Was there anything else?

Oh, yes, ...of course.

My heart.

If I asked to have it back,
would he be able to find it?

Might as well leave it at his place.

It's all battered and bruised now.

and anyway,
He won't even notice that it's there.

THIRTY AND A HALF

And just as i thought
i was getting old
and Springs would only be
bookmarks in my thoughts

You came along

to show me
the best is not yet to come
the best part of love
of life
is here
and now.

PRAYER FOR AN APARTMENT

Dear Lord,

Please forgive me
for all these lies I just done tol'.
Well, they wasn't exactly lies. . . .
Yeah, they was lies, Lord,
but Lord, you understand.

I couldn't never get no bigger apartment
in New York
If I told the truth!!

He be wantin' to know
where I worked
how long I worked there
what did I do
where I worked before that
where did I live
how long I been livin' there
and why was I leavin'
and why do I need four rooms in this apartment
I'm tryin' to git out of him——
and what was I gonna do with'em!!

Now, Lord, it's a nice apartment.
It's got——well, Lord
you know what it looks like.
Yeah. . . . . . .
it's nice, ain't it?

Now that I done tol' all these lies, Lord
Please protect me from them——
Don't let none of'em catch up to me.

Hey, Lord. If everything's cool,
and you take care of your end,
We be movin' next Saturday.

Amen.

'72 / West End Ave. phone booth
New York City

COME, MY BROTHER

(for Kwaanza)

Come, my Brother, give me your hand,
I want to lend it to a needin' man.

Come, my Sister, give me your hand,
You've got the strength to grow, I know you can.

Everybody's got to find his own way
To make this thing work out right.
Everybody here has something to say,
But we won't get it together if we fight, fight, fight!
Yebo!

Everybody's got a talent or two——
A gift from the gods to you.
Everything you learn you have to pass on,
If we put it all together we'll be strong, strong, strong!
Yebo!

Come, my children, give me your hands,
Let me teach you so you'll understand.

Come, my Brother, give me your hand,
I want to lend it to a needin' man.

'73 / The East, Brooklyn
New York City

ALFONZO WASHINGTON

VARNETTE P. HONEYWOOD

CLASSICAL MODERN

hot summer sun down

eyes caught on the nightlight backdrop

ears focused on the Philharmonic—

Tchaikowsky and rosé Symphony #5

in E minor giggling babies

floating through Sangria and bagels and

lovers and breathless air

Eyes touched on 2

moving through the meadow's bodies

badd bros in

white under/only/wear

with ripped sleeves

showing shining shoulders

draped in sweatbands

armed in armpits with tambourines

apple hats angled at near 90 degrees off left

to keep the heat of the moon

from burning their cool.

I mean,

you couldn't tell them that they weren't

sheet music for our eyes

As they swayed out of the park

I knew that

Roy notwithstanding

assimilation

was still a longer way off.

'74 / Central Park
New York City

GRACE WILLIAMS

ATMOSPHERE

he balanced his coffee
in one filthy hand
used cigarette stub
burning the other
and when she
brushed him lightly
he
jerked the crowd
with his scream

KEEP YOUR
FUCKIN' HANDS
OFF ME!!
DON'T TOUCH ME SHIT

but then I considered
that
the space around him
may be all
that he possesses
in this world

July, 1975 / Sixth Ave.
New York City

NEW YORK EXODUS

Sweet bird of freedom,

Touch me.

Sweet bird of freedom,

Fly away with me.

I'm gone!

Sweet bird of freedom,

Touch me.

Sweet bird of freedom,

Fly away with me.

I'm gone!

April 16, 1976
Kennedy Airport

360°

. . . AND THIS CHILD WILL BE SAFE . . .

AND THIS CHILD WILL BE FREE . . .

AND THIS CHILD WILL BE BLESSED

CHANGES, MY MAN?!

Changes, my man?
Did I hear you say
What I thought you said
That I'm puttin' a hurtin' on your head
By putting you through changes?
Me? Who's only been here
A quarter of a century?

You were changed by strangers
From a free man standing tall with me
To a chattel piece bent to your knees.
You had gods in abundance,
One for each need,
But now you speak of the Trinity.
Changes, my man?

Changes?
Did I just hear
What I thought I heard?
That I'm becoming a problem in your world
'Cause I'm putting you through changes?
Me? Who was
Designed to be your queen?

You were changed by southern belles
Who rang your father's funeral bell
And men who passed the time of day
By raping your mother
And disowning the product because of color.
Now you carry gardenias on your arm
And tell me that you mean no harm:
You simply make love to the enemy
In the name of political expediency.
Changes, my man?

VARNETTE P. HONEYWOOD

Changes?
Was than an alibi
Or an outright lie
When you said that I was "cramping your style"
And putting you through changes?
Me? a rose
In the garden of your destiny?

You have had your rhythm changed
From the dance of life by drums
To the dancebeat of the needle's plunge.
You have had your birthrate altered
From life giving stance
To drooping handed swish.
You question who you are,
And your children aren't too sure, either,
Yet you say I'm putting you through changes?

Changes, my man?!
because I ask for your time?
because your well being stays on my mind?

Changes, my man?!
because I don't want you calling me bitch again?
because I also want to be your friend?

Changes, my man?!
because I won't let you dwell on negative things?
because I believe you can do better?

Changes?
because I want you?
because I need you?
because I love you?
you say I'm putting you through changes?
changes, my man?
changes?
it changes,
it changes,
i say it changes
it changes
it has got to change
it has got to change
has to change
has to change,
has to change,
has to change. . . . .

WARNING!

some blue/black
brown determined-minded
soft touchin'
strong thinkin'
loud lovin'
pretty smilin'

KINSHASHA CONWILL

big eatin'
gentle teasin'
honey kissin'
eyes twinklin'
sweet brown
love man
betta come get me!
quick!

THE REASON BEING

I want to co-direct sunsets over root beer floats
someone to take me to the fair
to bake sweet potatoe pies
and chocolate chip cookies
for someone not on a diet

I want someone to explain football to me (again)
a broad brown back
to practice my tingling piano on
a house
with a built-in bear hug at the front door
and long Sunday mornings makin' love to My lord

I want someone in the audience on opening nights
a shoulder to enclose me after the last show

I want to argue politics madly
and make laughter
with the same smiles I use to make love

I want to feel that it's all right
to need the someone I need

I want a warm place to curl up in

And when I get it,
I want to dance
I want to dance to the music
without the music
I want the music maker
who makes the music
that makes me dance!

I want clear love
increasing love
want love with tenure
want a love supreme

And the only reason I'm still hangin' around
Is to see if they're gonna let me get down
Let me have
what I need to
got to
got to have

'cause that's the reason being

TOM FEELINGS

CAN YOU TEACH LOVE?

Maybe I was wrong,
Maybe I was foolish to think that
I could teach someone to love.

I thought that I was strong,
Strong enough to mold a child
Into a man. That was my plan.

Can you teach someone to love?
Is it possible to put things in a heart
That may not be there?
Can they grow there?

Did I try enough?
Did I hold back love
Or did I give too much?

Did I say things
In a way that he could understand
What it means to be a man?

Can you teach someone to love?
Can you show a boy that
It's all right to feel,
That gentleness is real?

Can you teach someone to love?
Is it possible to put things in a heart
That may not be there?
Can they grow there?
Can you teach someone to love?

(from The Sistuhs)

NESTING

Make a nest
a love nest

feather it
feather it with patience
learn to wait
avoid feeling the small hurts
feather it with gifts of love
but do not overgive

feather it with softness
soft evenings
soft poems
soft you
be the ultimate diversion
(from TV)

feather it with laughter
your smile so shines
that it's absence is regretted

feather it with vibes
of love
of getting there
of knowing/
learning
good cookin' vibes
flyin' high with
sweet wine & love time vibes

Make a nest
a love nest

then wait,

for the sweet wild one
to find his way home.

GRACE WILLIAMS

CHANGING SPACES

I do not want to be in that love posture
with you again.

I do not want to be seen coming into a
room on your arm again.

This is nothing personal.

An exercise has been performed here,
expertly executed
but void of emotion.

(I breathe on emotion)

I shift now, as the shadows,
But unlike the shadows, I will not come again,
in early morn, or sundown
or moonup, or on your face

My third sense tells me when I no longer belong
in a place/ a space,

And I move quickly to move swiftly from it.

You are one of those spaces.

You do not understand.
I can not explain.

I'm looking for another space to be
until my voices tell me
to move on,
or to stay,

I'm home.

LONESOME AND LONELY AIN'T THE SAME

Lonely is
walking around tryin' to look like the morning after
when there wasn't no night before

Lonesome is
having something good happen
(like hitting the number)
(or getting back a quarter from the pay phone)
and wanting to share the news
Lonely is
having no one to tell

Lonesome is
doing your ironing on Saturday night
instead of Saturday afternoon

Lonesome is
talking back to your television
Lonely is
talking back to your television when it isn't on

Lonely is
lying next to you,
wondering if that's where I should be?

Lonesome is
sleeping on one side of an empty bed
Lonely is
telling folks you can't sleep good
unless you're by yourself

Lonesome is
reading a book without seeing the words

Lonesome is
counting the days
Lonely is
trying to ignore the nights

Lonesome is
watching Lawrence Welk without realizing it

Lonesome is
when blues songs sound like love songs
Lonely is
when all blues songs sound like they were
written for and about you

Lonesome and Lonely ain't the same,
One's sweet, the other is pain.

Tim was killed today.

. . . .And I returned to thinking that being is about something far greater than the job, the rent $, freeway traffic, clocks, even Stevie's music.

It is all so much smaller and simultaneously so much bigger than we are. Because we cannot see our relative size, we expend a profusion of energy on/with/over nugatory moments and tangible needs that are indifferently minute within the larger scheme of the larger rhythm of our existence on this planet earth. We are simply passing through here. . . .

If that greater something is defined as love or as peace or as joy or as a warm feeling, then so be it. Whatever it is, there is no sense in being alive without it, and anything less is insignificant.

And are the gods to be commended or condemned for not letting those who loved Tim know that this would be their last day together? Would it have been better/easier/warmer to know? (A thought to be pondered.)

I pray that Tim and his lady had a tender moment for each other before they parted this morning; that he and his daughter shared some time/space of playful affection, or of teaching, or of silence together, that she will remember the moment and know that in her Daddy she was blessed with love.

It is the gift with which we are most challenged, both in the giving and the receiving.

Tuesday, September 6, 1977

SYLVIA M. MILLER

PASSING THROUGH

Man with his toy called war
Fights 'cause he has to have more
Men who don't agree
Keep each other from being free
Children go from door to door
Robbing the weak and the poor
Babies die of need
While politicians spread their greed

If I ever get free from here
Ain't comin' back again
If I ever get through that final door
Wouldn't come here no more!

The days, my heart near bursts with tears
Go to bed early to sleep away
the hours, the years, the fears
The loneliness is too much to bear
Sweet memories——aren't that many there
I've been forced to stay and endure the pain
But if I ever get off of here
Ain't comin' back again.

If I ever get my ass off this planet
And back where I began
Then I won't never (in any form)
Come back here again!

MEMORIAL PARTY

When I leave I want you to know
That this is exactly how I want to go:

Don't bury me down under, in a box sealed tight
'Cause I might not be able to get out at night.

Just broil the bod lightly, but don't season with tears
'Cause I had enough of them while I was here.

And damn! don't put the ashes in a jar on a shelf——
I'd make everyone nervous with the dust of myself!

Just spread them in places where the fires have been hot,
Let me blend with the embers of forget-me-not.

Then send out the invites to a celebration supreme,
To gather the best that I've known and seen;

The places and faces that created a smile
Will come together for one more good vibe.

I want you to party   hey, hey!
party   hey, hey!
party   hey, hey!
party   yebo!

Music is the first thing on a party's mind———
Aretha will fill that bill just fine,

Anything she wants to sing will be quite fair,
She got the music in me, and I'll be right there.

With Count Basie at the keyboard and Joe Williams at the door,
Let someone whirl my dancin' shoes out on the floor;

Collect the Clevelanders from Adams and Glenville High
To bring back the Swing that never went out of style.

Ernie Andrews and Lou Rawls should sing my blues,
Then Carmen and Nancy will fill in the other hues,

Put Danny (if you can catch him) in charge of the band
Then "With These Hands" Les McCann can.

When you're cooling your feet from the toe-tapping beats
You can have a seat under The Learning Tree,

While all of my mommas——and I've got quite a few——
Get loose in the kitchen over a party stew.

The gossip will flow and they'll do a little singin',
They'll put up a fuss, but those pots will be ringin'!

Have Dance Theatre, "Suite Otis," and others their style
Take the stage grandly for a little while.

Jamison, Ailey and their Black swans of dance
Will make a "Revelation" on what it means to prance!

Gather the girls from Dolly! for a chorus line,
And run the reels on Minstrel Man one last time.

Have Killens and Toni M. make fine note of it all,
And when it's time to change partners, Farrakhan will give the call.

I want you to pah-tee   sa-sa!
pah-tee   sa-sa!
pah-tee   sa-sa!
pah-tee   sa-sa!

The Wilmington 10, and the struggler's all
Will be free to answer the party roll call.

Stevie will sing something right in the groove,
While Varnette and Tom Feelings capture the mood.

Write Malcolm's warnings all over the wall
Remembering when we first became aware of the call.

You got to taste the sound of Sweet Honey In The Rock,
Then let diva Leontynne take it out at the top.

Let each of my Uncles get in one last tease.
Light seven candles for the peace of The East.

One more time, before I take flight,
Let me hear Linda Hopkins sing "Deep In The Night."

Line up the congas, do one dance on the drum,
And before it's all over, you got to give the Poets some!

This!
is!
your!
last!
chance!
to! par-teh with me
par-teh for me
par-teh get down!
par-teh get down!

Now, I've been very independent, never asked for much help,
But it's possible I won't be able to dispose of myself.

So I'm counting on those I leave gently behind
To honor my word, and have a part(y)ing good time!!

THERE ARE SOME THINGS. . . .

There are some things that cannot be put into poems.

Should not be.

Things I can't put on paper.

The empty frustration and wonderment and loss I feel every time I watch/see a black homosexual "doing his thing." There are no poetic terms for that. Not for that act, that state of being. Not for the pain I feel because of it.

There are some things that never come out in the right rhythm. You, when you are drunk, for one. Or him, when he asked if I loved him, and I could not find any answer. A young sister on the right path going in the wrong direction, whom I can't reach sufficiently to turn around, and so we barely speak. (And could I tell her the right things, if we did?) (And would she listen?)

There are small things, life's unpoetical annoyances, like cigarette smokers, new graffiti on a new wall, reaching to call you and finding the phone isn't working. Again.

I've tried to write about the "future generation" of the 70's, in their speckled high heeled sneakers, transistor radios welded to their wrists. Things that cannot be recorded in rhyme, even though they are of our time.

And things that will not be poems sometimes elate, often depress me. So I go to bed and dream and wake, willing to start all over again. Perhaps, beginning with a poem. . . . .

CONTENTS